GRANADA

Generalife. Patio de la
Acequia

Alhambra. Salón de Embajadores

FRANCISCO PRIETO-MORENO

GRANADA

EDITORIAL NOGUER, S. A.

BARCELONA - MADRID

English translation by
JOHN FORRESTER

Photographs by

CAMPAÑÁ-PUIG FERRÁN, CIGANOVIC, PIX, MIGUEL SÁNCHEZ,
SALMER and ZERKOWITZ.

CONTENTS

Alhambra. Sala de las
Camas

Alhambra. Patio de los Arrayanes

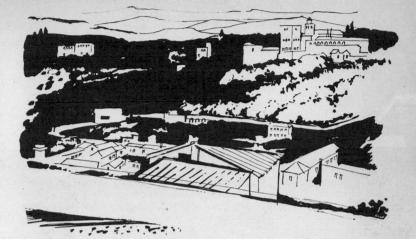

THE MAGIC OF GRANADA

General notions on Granada

It is indeed true that a city owes is character to those who built it and lived within its walls. In Granada, the geographical situation, the climate and the surrounding country are the basic elements which during long centuries have imperceptibly moulded the lives of its inhabitants, and influenced their ways of living and building. For this reason, the visitor who comes to Granada should not expect to find archaeological ruins on all sides; rather will he find himself in a living atmosphere which is the delight of the soul and the senses. The Grenadine region consists of a coast which is everywhere accessible to Mediterranean invaders, and a mountain range from which such invaders can sucessfully defend themselves against counter attacks from the hinterland beyond. Thus, this world in miniature, from its *Sierra* —the highest in all Spain— descending to the fertile lands of the broad plain and the tropical richness of its coastal strip, has been the scene of the longest epochs of influence of each of the incoming civilizations.

7

From the primitives to the Arabs

The Grenadine coast probably saw the arrival of prehistoric men during the Iron Age and the Bronze Age; the primitive mines of these settlers became known to the Phoenicians, who established their trading centre at Sexi, now Almuñecar, a port of call on the route to Gades. It is to the Roman occupation that we must turn if we wish to regard the mute evidence of the city's ancient foundation. Bridges and roads point to the passing of the Romans, as does the initial layout of the irrigation system, which the Arabs were to develop so extensively and with such consummate skill in a later epoch. It was with the complete overthrow of the Visigoth monarchy by the rushing tides of the Arab invasions however, that the real history of Granada was to begin. Those Moors who, impelled by their religious beliefs, swept in wave after wave from the hot sands of Africa, to vanquish the Visigoth resistance and consolidate their conquest ith the creation of the mighty Cordoban Caliphate, were for a time the veritable heirs of the *Imperium Mundi,* and as such, they felt the need for a manner of expressing the cultural influence of their dominion that would proclaim the magnificence of their civilization to succeeding ages. In the latter part of this epoch of Moorish dominion, the Arabs had lost their first pure faith in their destiny, and gave themselves up to more sensual delights and the luxurious pleasures of extreme refinement; this spirit was translated in terms of a completely unfettered architectural style, where the hard, uncompromising lines of carved stone gave way to the softer, more adaptable constructions of plaster, employed in a supreme outpouring of imaginative creation.

From the Reconquest to our times

This is the artistic phenomenon which occurred in Granada in the apogée of the Nazarite dynasty [1], a movement which only ended with the reconquest of the city by the Catholic Sovereigns [2] towards the end of the 15th Century. From then on, successive Spanish monarchs further embellished the last Moslem capital in the Peninsula, creating a new urban settlement at the foot of the hills on which rise the royal palace and the Arab city, facing one another. This modern city, dominated by its fine

[1] *Nazarite dynasty:* The Moslem dynasty which reigned in Granada from the 13th century until the 15th was so called after founder, Yusuf ben Nazar. [2] Fernando (1474-1516) and Isabel (1474-1504). During their joint reign the unity of Spain was achieved and America was discovered.

8

Cathedral, is itself a repository of the History of Art, with its superb monuments, the work of Renaissance, Baroque and neo-Classic masters. But above all, the outstanding feature of Granada is its atmosphere.

THE CHARACTER OF GRANADA

Intimate life and famous names

Granada is a tranquil city, almost static, the spirit of contemplation. The Grenadine is unable to adapt himself to the bustle of modern life; his sensitive spirit responds rather to the brilliant tones of the gardens, the contrasting shades of the nearby countryside. His ear is the sharper for listening to the song of innumerable nightingales, to the soothing murmur of the cool water as it babbles along the irrigation conduits or casts its dazzling spray into the air from the jets of countless fountains. Painting and Music both show the aesthetic influences exercised by Granada on its people. To cite but some of the great masters who have sprung from this soil, we would mention López Mezquita, Morcillo, Rodríguez Acosta, Falla and Andrés Segovia [1], though is should also be remembered that every villa has painter, and a guitar with which the family passes hours of intimate enjoyment. By the continual gentle exercise of such influences, Granada has produced writers and poets of the calibre of Ángel Ganivet and Federico García Lorca [2].

The Grenadine house. Patios and gardens

Maybe the Grenadine house reflects this peculiarity of its people more than does anything else. Here, however small the dwelling, it inevitably has a patio in the centre, where intimate friends are cheerfully welcomed, and where the family pass the greater part of their time; the patio serves to isolate the household from the outer world, yet without cutting them off from Nature, lavishly represented by a profusion of potted shrubs and flowers, while water tinkles musically in an ornamental basin. Writers who known Granada invariably set the action of their stories in the

[1] José María López Mezquita, b. 1883 in Granada, a renowned contemporary portrait painter. Gabriel Morcillo, b. 1891, notable Spanish painter. José María Rodríguez Acosta, b. 1878 in Granada, a notable Spanish painter. Manuel de Falla (1876-1946), one of the outstanding figures of contemporary Spanish music. Andrés Segovia, b. 1894, one of the outstanding concert guitarists of our day. [2] Angel Ganivet (1862-1898), a son of Granada and a noted Spanish thinker. Federico García Lorca (1899-1936), renowned Spanish poet and dramatist.

9

patios of the houses, and the influence of such customs on daily life is so great that even on notable fiestas, such as Corpus Christi, the balconies are adorned with hangins and with copper utensils, while the streets are covered with awnings and strewn with fragrant sedges. Even when a house stands on its own land, although this may be used for utilitarian purposes it is never allowed to lose its aspect of being yet another extension to the main patio. The ordered cultivation of the garden blends imperceptibly with the rich profusion of the orchard, following a truly oriental sense of harmony. Patio and garden both serve as settings for small gatherings of intimate friends, where the keen critical faculty of the Grenadine is brought into play in the discussion of countless aspects of cultural life. Not infrequently, such groups will end up by leaving the garden, to continue the discussion as they take a leisurely stroll, stopping from time to time to admire the golden glow of the setting sun as it illumines first one, then another feature of the landscape. In this way, a strong tradition is maintained, calling to mind the '98 generation of intellectuals —*Los de la cuerda granadina*— thronging around Ganivet on the road to the *Fuente del Avellano* [1].

Craftsmanship

This same aesthetic sense which has produced such masters in all the spheres of Art has also developed an ancient tradition of fine craftsmanship in many old skills, the Grenadines being especially famous for their wonderful embroideries and carpets, copperware, wrought iron ware and marquetry.

Public institutions

Not the least remarkable however, is the fact that though such pursuit of artistic pre-eminence would seem to have shut off Granada from the rest of the world, such is not the case, and side by side with its artistic achievements we have a record of constant and decisive influences exercised on Spanish history and culture. Among its more famous sons who have played their part in the broader realm of national affairs, we must mention Archbishop Talavera [2], and the renowned Marqués de Mondéjar, first Captain-General of Granada, an office that was also to be occupied by Gonzalo de Córdoba, the *Gran Capitán* [3], one of the most stirring

---

[1] *Los de la cuerda granadina* was the name bestowed on the group of literary men presided over by Angel Ganivet, which used to meet in the *Fuente del Avellano*. [2] Hernando de Talavera (1428-1507), confesor and counsellor to the Catholic Queen, and author of important didactic treatises. [3] Gonzalo Fernández de Córdoba, famous Spanish general, called *El Gran Capitán* (1453-1515).

figures of mediaeval history. In its own sphere, the University has ever been in the forefront of Spanish seats of learning. Thus Granada, as the busy centre of a fertile agricultural region, besides maintaining its traditional pre-eminence in the aesthetic field, has played an increasingly active part in the economic development of Spain.

ITINERARIES

In orden to know all the diverse aspects of Granada, and to appreciate its distinct historical, artistic and popular values, a stay of some day in the city is necessary. However, as some visitors travel on a restricted timetable, we would also point out that it is possible to see the places of outstanding interest in one day. If a traveller is staying in one of the hotels of the Alhambra, he should spend the morning, from nine till twelve, visiting the Arab Palace, the Palace of Carlos V and the rest of the precincts, afterwards descending to the city for a tour of its central monumental edifices, the *Corral del Carbón* and the *Casa de los Tiros*. Lunch could be eaten in a typical restaurant in town, and the afternoon spent visiting the *Cartuja,* the *Albaicín,* the Provincial Museum and the Chancellery, later going up to the Generalife, from where the wonderful effects of the sunset over the city and the *Sierra* can be admired. After dinner is a good time go along to the Caves on the *Sacromonte,* to watch a gipsy *zambra.* Staying in the city, naturally it is better for a visitor to pass the morning visiting the monuments in town and the Cartuja and the *Albaicín,* leaving all the afternoon free for the Alhambra and the Generalife.

I. *The Alhambra*

Vegetation, the birds and the water
In former times a fortress enclosing the Palace and Court apartments of the Grenadine kings, the Alhambra is today a garden, in which the landscape and the luxurious growth of the vegetation are the dominant features. We start our stroll at the *Puerta de las Granadas,* from which we make our way up a steep slope, among the rich greenery of the wood, the natural, and even wild appearance of which is but a foretaste of some the marvels of

11

Nature we shall later contemplate. It is pleasant walking under the shade cast by the huge trees, with here and there a small pool of light where the sun breaks through the foliage; on all sides we can hear the chirping of birds, and the soft murmur of running water as it follows its course down the hill from the gardens and patios of the Arab Palace.

Outer view of the Alhambra

This path passes the first monumental landmark on our way the great *Pilar de Carlos V,* a piece of sculpture that is pure Italian Renaissance in style, and seems to initiate a conflict of civilizations that we shall continually notice in the Alhambra. Just a little farther ahead, we come to the imposing mass of the *Puerta de la Justicia,* with its entrance at right angles; the inscriptions above it dedicate all that is defended within these walls to Allah and to Mohammed, his Prophet. We have now the *Plaza de los Aljibes,* a broad promenade, on the left of wich rises the *Alcazaba,* the main defence of the Alhambra, dominated by the *Torre de la Vela,* over which the standard of the Catholic Sovereigns was unfurled when the city was reconquered. To the right, we can see the PALACE OF CARLOS V and the ARAB PALACE.

Panorama from the mirador

But before penetrating any of these buildings, it might be a good idea to go over to the mirador in the background, from where one can gaze out over the whole extensive panorama of the *Albaicín,* which covers the opposite hill on the other side of the Darro. Looking out sideways, rather in the manner of getting a bird's eye view, we can make out many details of the complex pattern of houses, convents, churches, orchards, and gardens which together form this enchanting mediaeval town, with its winding streets and its hidden little squares, shady and inviting. The very sight of this apparent city in miniature, with its rich profusion of diverse elements, seems to exercise a hypnotic effect, but even more intriguing is the wave of sound borne up on the air from the *Albaicín* towards the Alhambra. The acoustics of this natural depression are so perfect that the clear air carries every little sound to our ears —the cries of the children at play, the hawkers shouting their wares, and the steady buzz of conversation. The sweet fragrance of the flowers bestows the last, perfect note on this scene as we feast our eyes on the unforgettable view of the *Albaicín* and the gipsy *Sacromonte.*

Alhambra. Patio de los Leones

Alhambra.
Pórtico del Partal

Alhambra. Hall of Kings

Origins and characteristics of the construction

Now indeed can we make our way to the Arab Palace of the Alhambra with our spirits tuned to its bewitching air. The fortified precincts of the Alhambra comprise three sections formed by the *Alcazaba,* the Royal Palaces and the Citadel. King Alhamar, the first monarch of the Nazarite dynasty, decided in 1238 to remove his Court to this fortified hill from the *Albaicín,* where it had formerly been installed. His successors followed in his steps, influenced in their decisions no doubt by the necessity of having a means of defence against the Christian incursions into their territory, which by that time were becoming ever more daring; at the same time, the fortified walls gave protection to the reigning sovereign in the event of civil or dynastic disturbances in the kingdom itself. The main buildings were constructed during the 14th century in the reigns of Yusuf I and Mohamed V [1]. The Alhambra is therefore one of the last achievements of a Moslem monarchy which was accustomed to living side by side with Christians, and even to reigning in vassalage to Castilian sovereigns, to whom they had paid annual tributes for many years. The Oriental tradition is here seen to be blended with a mediaeval style which is on the verge of becoming Renaissance, yet over all can be noticed philosophical characteristics that are strongly Arabic. The Alhambra combines in its edifices a number of architectural values which are still effective today, and indeed are considered to be masterpieces. We can easily observe the skilful use of Nature in the planning of the buildings, getting the fullest possible advantage from the position, and letting the vegetation penetrate to the most intimate corners, thus carrying the project to the very extreme of naturalism. The ground plan, free and open, yet retaining a very firm nucleus centred on the patio; the austere forms, with perspectives superimposed, creating transparencies that are not dissimilar to those of cubism, could truly serve as a lesson for the most advanced of modern designers. In the same way, in the construction itself, we notice that the technique employed called for the complete elimination of the massive thickness which is a feature of classical edifices, producing a pile that is wonderfully light. Yet the passage of centuries has shown that the Alhambra is one of the strongest, most resistant monuments known in History, in spite of being composed of some of the most fragile materials ever used for monumental construction.

[1] Yusuf I, King of Granada (1330-1354). Mohamed V, King of Granada (1354-1391).

13

The North side of the Alhambra, overlooking the Valley of the Darro, in which can be appreciated the blending of the military architecture of the towers and the civil lines of the palaces with the vast green mass of the woods. The existence of the interior garden is outlined by the sharp fingers of the cypreses

Such a result has only been achieved by a masterly use of such materials, as is shown by the marble pavements, the delicate plasterwork in the upper parts, protected where necessary by overhanging eaves.

The Arab Palace

In the Arab Palace of the Alhambra can be remarked three distinct sections, which nevertheless from a perfectly unified functional whole though each is quite independent of the others and designed to fulfil its particular use only. The administration of the Court was centred in the *Mexuar*, where also was the court of justice, while political and legislative life was controlled from the *Cuarto de Comarex*. The *Patio de los Leones* was the heart of the monarch's private apartments, and formed a part of the harem quarters.

The Mexuar

Nowadays, the palace is entered via the *Mexuar,* the first room to be visited being a hall where four colums set in the centre carry bow-shaped corbels which supported a higher structure, this latter having been pulled down in the reign of Felipe V [1]. The walls are extensively decorated with fine plasterwork, and with tiled socles in which heraldic emblems of the Nazarite monarchs are intermingled with those of Carlos V [2] and the Mendoza

[1] Felipe V, King of Spain (1700-1746). [2] Carlos I of Spain and V of Germany (1517-1556). The greatest King-Emperor of his time.

14

family. This hall, which in the Moorish times was Council Chamber and Royal Audience Hall, was converted into a chapel in the 14th Century. At the far end, looking out over the Darro and the *Albaicín* we have the Moslem *Oratory,* facing the East, with its richly adorned Koranic niche, this having been built in the reign of Mohammed V.

The Comarex Palace

This part of the palace is linked with the *Palacio de Comarex* by a patio which could almost be considered as miniature, yet it was not thought to be too small to be further embellished with a lovely fountain. We come now to the royal apartments, and on the north side of this patio we can see the *Cuarto Dorado,* over which were the lodgings of the Christian governors of the Alhambra, while on the south side we have the *Cuarto de Comarex,* in the façade of which, under a superb carved wooden gable, are two doors set in glazed tile lintels. The heraldic emblems of the Nazarite dynasty are one of the main motifs of the plaster decoration here also, as in practically all of the palace. Passing through these doors, we reach the patio of the *Cuarto de Comarex,* more commonly known as the *Patio de los Arrayanes,* on account of the myrtle growing around the pool. At the far ends of the patio are the porticos, faced by seven arches resting on marble columns, and in the lateral naves we can contemplate a series of twin-arched windows on the upper floor, which were given over to the women's apartments.

We pass though the centre portico, under the *Torre de Comarex* and enter the *Sala de la Barca,* a name that is derived either from the Arab work *baraka,* meaning "blessing", which we see extensively repeated in the mural decorations, or from the shape of its ceiling, which does to some degree resemble a boat. A rather interesting feature of this room is the series of niches at each side of the entrance arch, where vases of flowers were placed. The vaulting of the *Sala de la Barca* was destroyed in a fire which occurred towards the end of the 19th Century. Continuing our visit, we pass on to the *Salón de Embajadores,* where was the Throne. It was in this hall that the Council met and decided to surrender Granada to the Christian forces, and it is thought that here too was the scene of the discussions which led to the concluding of the agreement between the Catholic Sovereigns and Christopher Columbus that was to result in the discovery of the New World. The entire rooms is adorned with fine plasterwork, bearing religious inscriptions singing the praises of King Yusuf I, and the roof is composed of a wonderful cedarwood dome, profusely adorned with bows and stars. The little anteroom on the right of the *Salón de Embajadores* leads down to the *Baths*, very similar in their layout to the old Roman baths.

The Private Residence and the Patio de los Leones
Our way now leads us up to the *Patio de los Leones* and the adjoining apartments, a part of the Palace that was given over entirely to the king's private life. Built by order of Mohammed V, this section of the Alhambra corresponds to the last epoch of its construction. Set around this famous patio we have a number of fine halls: the *Sala de los Mocárabes* [1] to the West; the *Sala de los Reyes*, to the East; the *Sala de Dos Hermanas*, the *Ajimeces* and the *Mirador de Lindaraja*, to the North; and the *Sala de los Abencerrajes*, to the South. The longer sides of the patio open on to the *Sala de los Abencerrajes* and the *Sala de Dos Hermanas* through semicircular arches, while on the shorter sides we have the two pavilions, roofed over in the interior with wooden domes and fine lattice work. The vaulting of the *Sala de los Mocárabes* disappeared towards the end of the 16th Century. The great marble slabs set in the centre of the paving have given its name to the *Sala de Dos Hermanas*, though the most beautiful feature of this room is its superb bow-worked dome, one of the loveliest in the whole palace. Delicate plaster decorations entirely cover the walls, the inscriptions being in praise of Allah and of King Mohamed V, while a fountain graces the centre of the floor. Two little alcoves can be seen at the sides. We pass under the middle arch to enter the *Sala de los Ajimeces*, which leads us to the *Mirador de Lindaraja*.

On the other side of the patio lies the *Sala de los Abencerrajes*, where tradition would have us believe were beheaded the thirty-six knights of the noble Moslem family after whom the hall is named; unvouched for by history, this event seems to be linked with the reign of Mohammed X [2]. The dome of this apartment is yet another example of the rich creative talents of the craftsmen who designed and decorated it, and its brow-working takes on new, contrasting tones as the light shines on it through one after

---

[1] *Mocárabes:* Ceiling adorned with ribbon worked wood. [2] Tradition relates that the *Sala de los Abencerrajes* was the scene of the execution by beheading of thirty-six knights from this Moslem tribe, by order of Mohamed X. Other accounts place this event in the reign of Muley Hacen, and yet others in the reign of Boabdil.

another of the seventeen windows. Finally, we come to the *Sala de los Reyes,* on the west side of the *Patio de los Leones,* a rectangular apartment to which three porticos give access. The hall is divided into three square rooms by double arches, the ceiling being richly vaulted. At the end of each of these rooms we can observe a niche, in the upper parts work of a late 14th Century Italian artist. The middle canvas portrays the first ten Nazarite monarchs, while the lateral painting depict scenes of chivalry, clearly showing the extent to which the Grenadine Arabs and the Christians had come to understand one another in the Middle Ages. A florid verse in praise of the King was written by Ibn Zamrek, and can be seen sculpted around the fountain of this enchanting patio.

Blessed be who granted to Iman Mohamed delectable mansions that for their beatuy are supreme among mansions. This is the garden; in it are works of such beauty that God has not permitted any other loveliness to compare with them, and the transparent brightness of the dewdrops decks the borders with a trimming of pearls.

Liquid silver that runs among the jewels, which has no fellow in whiteness and transparency.

Fluid and solid are blended in one, water and marble, and we cannot tell which of the two is in motion.

Don't you see how the water runs at the side, and yet later hides itself in the conduits?

Like a lover whose eyes are brimming with tears, which he hides for fear they betray him.

And in truth what is it, but a cloud which sheds its caresses over the lions!

Like the hand of the Caliph when he appears in the morning, casting his offering to his wild lions.

Oh, thou who regardest these lions that lie in wait; out of respect they dare not show their enmity!

Oh, heir of the Ansares, and not through an indirect line; heritage of grandeur by which thou despisest the mighty!

The peace of God be with thee for ever, be thy delights increased and thine enemies vanquished.

3

The stalactitic decorative schemes of the ceiling call to mind the image of the ordered lines of the royal tents before battle, pitched in front of a petrified forest of palm trees, a bubbling spring bursting from the ground.

Such an affirmation may seem a little exaggerated, yet it does convey the innate genius of the Arabs for incorporating Nature itself in rich architectural forms, which are in themselves the

Plan showing the natural inspiration of the *Patio de los Leones*

product of a refinement in the Moorish way of living in the centuries following the invasion of Spain.

The layout of the Palace of the Alhambra unequivocally expresses the Grenadine spirit, with its high regard for light, colour, vegetation and water, displaying to the full the most dazzling facet of each element.

The Patio de la Reja *and the* Patio de Lindaraja

Modifications effected after the Arab epoch brought into being other patios and gardens, which today form a part of the monumental ensemble; such additions are the *Patio de la Reja* and the *Patio de Lindaraja*. In the former of these, the cypresses, the fountain, the inner chamber communicating with the *Patio de Lindaraja* and the open portico all repeat the characteristics we have mentioned. From inside, the imposing sight of

18

the *Torre de Comarex*, the distant pattern of the *Albaicín*, and the close contact with water and vegetation combine in an effect that would stimulate the slowest imagination to rhapsodise over the peerless beauty of such a scene on a moonlit night.

The *Patio de Lindaraja* has the appearance of a cloister, with the apartments constructed for the use of the Emperor Carlos V enclosing it completely; these same rooms were later occupied by Washington Irving during his memorable stay in the Alhambra. Yet the very air of the place asserts that it too is inevitably bound to the Alhambra. During the Nazarite epoch, the garden lay between the Mirador known as *Ain-Dar-Axa* — "Eyes of the Palace of the Sultana"— and the distant panorama of the *Albaicín*. The depths to which these enchanted surroundings stirred the senses of the poets of past ages can be seen in the verses sculpted on the arches.

> *I am not alone, for a delightful garden can be contemplated from this spot.*
>
> *Such a place has never before been seen.*
>
> *This is the Crystal Palace; he who looks on it will believe he regards the mighty ocean and will be filled with fear.*
>
> *All this is the work of Imán Ibn Nasar, may God keep his grandeur for other kings.*
>
> *His forbears in ancient time were of the most noble, giving hospitality to the Prophet and his family.*

Around the arched windows through which the far horizon is discerned we can read another verse that describes even more fully the *Mirador de Lindaraja:*

> *Mohammed, glorified for his bravery and generosity, he of widespread renown, he of the upright mind.*
>
> *The guiding moon is resplendent on the horizon of the Empire, its signs are lasting and its splendour brilliant.*
>
> *He is a sun which has risen in this mansion, whose shadow even confers benefits.*
>
> *From here he regards the capital of the Empire from his magnificence on the Throne of the Caliphate.*

19

> *Casting his glance where the breezes play, contented*
> *with the honour they do him.*
>
> *These mansions are so entrancing to the sight that the*
> *vision enslaved and the intelligence overwhelmed.*
>
> *Here are made manifest the wonders of a crystal*
> *world.*
>
> *Beauty is engraved on all its surface, decking it with*
> *opulent splendour.*
>
> *Light and colour are each disposed in such a way that*
> *thou mayest consider them as distinct elements or as*
> *analogous material.*

Even the topmost basin of the fountain which graces the centre of the patio is employed to sing the praises of this wonderful spot, in another verse:

> *In truth am I a crystal world, that shows itself clearly*
> *to men, without a veil.*
>
> *A vas sea, whose confines are works of finest marble.*
>
> *And the water runs like liquid pearls. How wonderful!*
>
> *The water is taken from me in such a way that some-*
> *times I hide myself from thee.*
>
> *As if I and the running water were a piece of ice, part*
> *melting, part solid.*
>
> *As darkness falls thou wouldst belive me to be higher*
> *than the stars.*
>
> *My splendour like a shell, and those drops a heap of*
> *pearls!*

The Towers

At one time a separate entity, the *Torre del Peinador* was altered by the construction of the gallery which ruins round the lower body and which is now a magnificent vantage point; the alteration as carried out because the Empress' private apartments had been installed in the Tower during Carlos V's stay in the Alhambra.

Within the walled precincts, yet not forming part of the royal palace, a series of mansions housed the courtiers, these edifices being scaled-down copies of the regal pile. Falling into private hands after the Reconquest, they were gradually allowed to crumble and decay, only those of exceptional architectural merit

The lower garden of the Generalife

The Alhambra
with the Sierra Nevada
in the background

Alhambra. Palace of Carlos V

being conserved. In modern times, as excavation works have been completed, gardens have been laid out on the sites where remains of these old noble residences have come to light. This has happened in the case of the *Partal* and the *Secano,* which has acquired its primitive personality. The *Torre de las Damas,* or *Partal,* consists of a portico of five arches, set between a pool whose waters reflect the pavilion, and a small chamber, from where one can contemplate and admire the panorama over the Darro and the *Albaicín.* From the *Partal* start all the towers which nestle alongside the wall, beginning with the Mihrab, or domestic Oratory, and continuing with the *Torre de los Picos* the *Torre del Cadí,* and the *Torre de la Cautiva,* this latter named after the Christian favourite of Muley Hacén, doña Isabel de Solís, after this we have the *Torre de las Infantas,* an edifice that was built during the last years of the Arab domination, about 1450. The interior rooms of these two towers are sumptuously decorated. Yet another interesting feature of the *Torre de las Infantas* is the very romantic legend linked with this lovely building, recounted by Washington Irving. [1] Turning again towards the southern side of the precincts we come to the *Torre y Puerta de Siete Suelos,* in former times the most important entrance to the Alhambra, and the one through which it is supposed the Catholic Sovereigns made their entry into this magnificent pile.

The Palace of Carlos V and the Provincial Fine Arts Museum

The PALACE OF CARLOS V is a noble construction of the Renaissance period. The construction was started in 1526 by Pedro Machuca, painter and architect, a pupil of Michelangelo and Raphael. The buildings is a wonderful architectonic work, of well thought-out lines and fine ornamentation. The façades of this quadrangular construction consist of two bodies. The lower is in raised work and in the pilasters splendid bronze rings are inserted, fastened by eagle or lion heads. A row of square and another of circular windows complete the arrangement of this lower body. At the upper body there are circular windows and balconies alterating, in a similar fashion, with pilasters. The decoration, richer than on the lower body, is very remarkable.

The portals of the two principal façades, especially those of the

---

[1] The legend tells of the three princesses, Zaida, Zoraida and Zorahida, who fell in love with three Spanish knights. In spite of the vigilance of their father, Mohammed, *el Zurdo,* two of them managed to escape from the tower with their lovers. The third's courage failed her at the last minute and she remained to die of grief in the tower that now bears their name.

southern façade, are very beautiful. The design of this portal was made by Machuca and the sculptural work was done by Nicolao de Corte. On the portal of the western façade magnificent bas-reliefs may be admired, the work of Juan de Orea, according to designs made by Pedro Machuca. The interior court of yard is circular and has a diameter of 31 metres; it is enclosed by an ample portico of Doric colums. The upper part, of the same distribution, shows Ionic columns on a parapet, the pediment reposing upon these columns. The upper corridor has not been covered. Although the patio is somewhat marred by this fact, its beauty is unquestionable.

The PROVINCIAL FINE ARTS MUSEUM is installed in the upper part of the Carlos V Palace. The twelve rooms contain an important collection of sculptures and paintings, mostly from Granada, ranging from the end of the 15th Century to the present day. Particularly outstanding are: an enamel triptych by Nardón Pinicaud; sculptures by Jacobo Florentino, Siloé, Alonso Cano, Pedro de Mena, Mora, Diego de Aranda and Risueño; paintings by Sánchez Cotán, Carducho, Castillo, Arias, Alonso Cano, Pedro de Moya, Bocanegra, Juan de Sevilla, Risueño, Vicente López, Machazo, Gómez Moreno, Fortuny, Berruete, Rodríguez Acosta, López-Mezquita, Muñoz Degrain, Morcillo and Cossío.

II. *The* Generalife

Dominating panorama

We have intentionally recommended the visitor to try and arrange his trip to the *Generalife* immediately before sundown. Nowadays, the visitor makes his way into this wonderful estate along an imposing avenue of manificent cypresses, erect and motionless as a line of guards; although this drive breathes of the stately elegance of the eighteenth century, so far removed from the original idea of the Arab gardens, neverthless it is somehow quite in keeping with the spirit of Granada. Step by step we follow the ascending path, until we come to the slope on which the *Generalife* is situated, its breathtaking beauty dominating the Grenadine landscape. On one side, we have the old Moorish city of the *Albaicín,* with the Darro winding along its way down below; on the other, separated from this spot by the *Cuesta del Rey Chico,* the Alhambra, with all its towers, while in the centre

22

the Plain stretches away to the distant horizon, where it imperceptibly blends with the pure brilliance of the *Sierra Nevada*.

Origins of the Generalife

The GENERALIFE, a name which etymological authorities tell us means "Sublime Garden", was originally planned for the pleasure and recreation of the Arab monarchs, being connected with the Alhambra by a private way which started at the *Puerta de Hierro*, alongside the *Torre de los Picos*. The path followed by the kings was protected by the *castle* which is now known as *Santa Elena*, and possibly also by an extension of the fortifications.

Architecture and vegetation

Although its ground plan is a perfect study in proportions, the architecture of the *Generalife* seems to play a complementary role to the rich vegetation. Of the primitive buildings, the two pavilions situated at either end of the *Patio de la Ría* are outstanding, though seen from the exterior their size is not at once apparent; these pavilions, hidden by the foliage, strike the note of the formal architectural style. Nevertheless, their superb lines are controlled by the axis along which the whole composition is balanced, which can be noticed through the porticos of the main apartment, when one can see that in spite of all the luxurious decoration with which they were surrounded, the former royal inhabitants of this noble pile still delighted in the quiet contemplation of long perspectives of natural scenery. The gardens themselves are the ideal achievement of a place of quiet and isolation, from which one can look out over Granada, enlivened by the low murmur of sound rising from the *Albaicín*.

Various precincts

The *Generalife* is like a bracelet of precious jewels, each one faceted to show off to the best advantage its particular qualities; every apartment is designed and situated in accordance with ts recreational purpose. As one enters the very first patio, one is impressed by the function of this palace, for the entrance courtyard is intended to stable the mounts of those arriving, while the second is a portico leading to the main apartment. The *Patio de la Ría*, with its pavilions at either end situated along the axis defined by the line of the watercourse, is enlivened by the scintillating jets of the fountains, which turn one's gaze away to the right, towards the valley of the Darro and the *Albaicín*, and

23

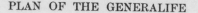

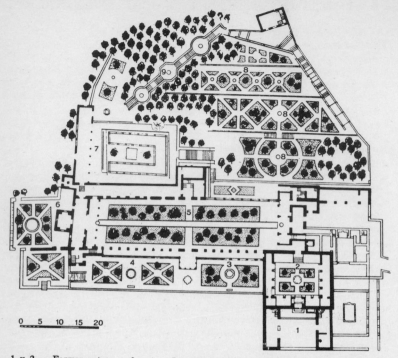

1 y 2. — Former entrance. 3 y 4. — Low garden. 5. — Patio de la Ría. 6. — Mirador. 7. — Patio of the Sultana's Cypress. 8. — High gardens. 9. — Staircase of the Cascades.

the contemplation of the Alhambra and the Plain. From here, we proceed to a yet more intimate spot, which gave rise to the legend of the *Sultana's Cypress*[1]. It is a place of complete spiritual concentration, where the water bursts forth in silvery streams, while the architectural features are reduced to simple walls, among which the cypresses, roses and oleanders, reflected a thousand times in the placid surface of the pool, bring a note of fragance and colour to the enchanted atmosphere. The ingeniously

[1] The legend relates that wife of the Emir Boabdil and a knight of the Abencerrajes held tryst under the so-called "Cypress of the Sultana". As a result, a the noble men of this tribe were beheaded.

planned upper garden, to which we ascend by a fantastic stairway, is a veritable apotheosis of Nature, blending with the surrounding scenery.

The water in the Generalife
The oldest description of the *Generalife* since the time of the Reconquest is that of Andrea Navaggiero, an Italian ambassador who visited this spot some thirty years after Granada had been retaken; his account gives us some idea of what the gardens must have looked like originally.

"There is water in all the palace, even within the apartments one patio that is entirely covered with greenery, like a lawn dotted ith trees, by shutting off some of the channels without the person on the lawn being aware of it, the water is made to rise under his feet, finally bursting through the lawn in countless fine jets, bathing the occupant's feet and cooling him in the summer heat. The water is made to rise and fall without any apparent effort whatever. Higher up, a garden encloses a wide, beautiful staircase and a small lawn, where is a certain stone controlling all the water which runs through the palace. In that place can be seen numerous valves, so that the water can be regulated to runs as it is required. The staircase is constructed in such a wey that at every few steps there is a landing, where the water collects, and the stonework adorning either side has its copings hollowed out like channels." This description serves to confirm the fundamental characteristics of the gardens in the Arab epoch.

But throughout this romantic place it is the water which confers the last gracious note, bringing life and emotion to the whole of the *Generalife*. Cascades, fountains and channels carry the precious liquid through the gardens, and on moonlit nights, wnen the vegetation and the buildings melt into the shadow, the silvery music of the running water creates a magical atmosphere, stirring the senses and calling up visions of past splendours in the mind's eye.

III. The City

Granada and national unity
A visit to the main places of artistic interest in the centre of the city will serve to make a visitor aware of the importance attached to Granada by the Catholic Sovereigns and by succes-

25

4

sive Spanish monarchs. Since the end of the 15th Century, Granada represented the victorious end of a great enterprise, and at the same time the flowering of a new era of political unity as the five ancient kingdoms of mediaeval Spain were brought together under one sceptre. The fifth kingdom, as Granada was considered to be, constituted the last internal link in the great monarcny founded by Ferdinand and Isabella. The consummation of this newly won unity was bound to be expressed joyously in all the arts, as we can see from all the monuments of the epoch, among which are included the Royal Chapel, founded by the Catholic Sovereings to serve as their last resting place, and the Cathedral.

The Royal Chapel

The Royal CHAPEL was finished in the reign of Carlos V, and the mortal remains of the joint sovereings were laid to rest there, beign removed from their temporary sepulchre in the Convent of San Francisco de la Alhambra. The edifice is an example of the last period of Gothic architecture and is profusely adorned with shields bearing the initials of the Catholic Sovereigns, heraldic devices, pinnacles and gargoyles. In its interior, the outstanding feature is the magnificent grille, wrought by Bartolomé de Jaén in 1520 and considered to be the finest plateresque grille in all Spain; in the centre we can see a wonderfully worked heraldic scene, surmounted by Biblical episodes, the whole being crowned by a portrayal of Calvary. The tombs of the Catholic Sovereigns were carved from Carrara marble in Genoa by Domingo Fancelli. Adjoining them, on another sepulcre, we can regard the recumbent figures of doña Juana and don Felipe [1], also worked in the Italian style, by Ordóñez. As we contemplate the High Altar of the Chapel, we can admire the magnificent plateresque retable created by Felipe de Vigarny, together with the praying figures of the Catholic Sovereigns, attributed to Diego de Siloé. On the left of the transept we have a fine triptych of *La Pasión*, painted by Dierich Bouts, which, together with the altar panels by Hans Memling which can be seen in the sacristy, and other works by Botticelli, Van der Weyden, etc., formed part of the superb art collection owned by Queen Isabella.

The vaulting of the sacristy collapsed during the first half of the 19th Century, and was restored as nearly as possible to its original form in 1945. Here too are kept a number of relics of the

[1] Doña Juana, daughter of Isabel la Católica, proclaimed Queen of Castile in 1505, was married to the Archduke Felipe, son of Maximilian, Emperor of Austria.

The Royal Chapel. Royal sepulchres

The Cathedral. Main Chapel

Catholic Sovereigns, such as the Queen's crown and sceptre, and a chest and mirror which belonged to the illustrious monarch, King Fernando's sword, military plans for the Reconquest, and objects of great historical value.

The Choir, with its Gothic choirstalls and a great faldstool in the middle, is yet another example of artistic achievement; the panels of the faldstool are carved with figures of the Apostles which are also thought to be the work of Diego de Siloé. At the side, we have the Chapter Hall, installed in the upper storey, of the *Lonja de Mercaderes.*

The crypt is especially impressive, being bare of all adornment. Here in simple state lie the leaden coffins containing the remains of the Catholic Sovereigns, in accordance with their expressed wishes that after death they should not be surrounded by rich panoply and adornment.

The Cathedral

History of its construction

The original entrance to the Chapel now forms part of the CATHEDRAL, where we continue our visit. The site on which the Great Mosque of the city stood had been indicated by *Isabel la Católica* as the place where the Royal Chapel and the Cathedral were to be built. Work was not begun on this project until 1523, when the two master craftsmen commissioned with its execution, Hontañón and Egas, drew up designs for a Gothic construction, similar to the Cathedral of Toledo. Some five years later, Diego de Siloé took charge of the work, adapting the Gothic plans to the new Renaissance style. This great artist supervised the development of his plan for thirty-five years, in this time creating one of the outstanding Renaissance temples of the world; during this period, the head of the Cathedral, together with the tower and transept, were finished and made fit for worship. At the death of Siloé in 1563, his work was taken over a pupil, Maeda, who was in turn followed by Juan de Orea, Ambrosio de Vico, and Miguel Guerrero.

Main Façade

In 1667, Alonso Cano was appointed to take charge of the construction, his chief contribution to the sacred pile being its main façade, a veritable masterpiece, composed of three great arches, the middle one bigger than the others; built as a triumphal entrance, the vigorous lines of this composition are extremely impressive. Above the centre doorway we van admire a sculptured

PLAN OF THE CATHEDRAL AND ROYAL CHAPEL

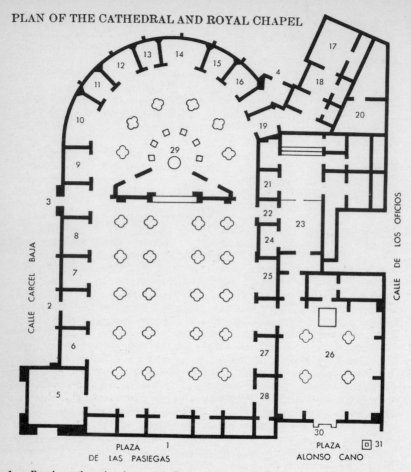

1. — Façade and main door. 2. — Door of Saint Jerónimo. 3. — Door of Pardon. 4. — Door of Ecce Homo. 5. — Cathedral Tower and Treasure. 6. — Chapel of Pilar. 7. — Chapel of Carmen. 8. — Chapel of the *Angustias.* 9. — Chapel of the Antigua. 10. — Chapel of Saint Lucía. 11. — Chapel of the Christ *de las Penas.* 12. — Chapel of Saint Theresa. 13. — Chapel of Saint Blas. 14. — Chapel of Saint Cecilio. 15. — Chapel of Saint Sebastián. 16. — Chapel of Saint Ana. 17. — Sacristy. 18. — Antesacristy. 19. — Sacristy Portal. 20. — Chapter Hall. 21. — Retable of Santiago. 22. — Main Royal Chapel Portal. 23. — Royal Chapel. 24. — Retable of Jesús the Nazarene. 25. — Chapel of the Trinity. 26. — Presbitery. 27. — Chapel of Saint Michael. 28. — Cathedral Museum. 29. — Great Chapel. 30. — Presbitery Main Door. 31. — Monument to Alonso Cano.

relief representing the "Mystery of the Incarnation", while the lateral entrances are adorned by reliefs of the "Visitation and Assumption of the Virgin". The upper part of the fronting is embellished with round and star-shaped louvers, and over the first cornice can be noticed scenes from the Old and New Testaments, and figures of San Rafael and San Miguel, these fine works being by Miguel and Luis Verdiguier. Two towers should have been built, one on each side of the façade, but of these, one never left the planning stage and the other was left unfinished; this latter is fifty-seven metres high and is formed of three groups, adorned with Doric, Ionic and Corinthian columns respectively. Work was about to be begun on the fourth and last group, but it was noticed that the earlier constructions were showing signs of decay, and it was decided to abandon the project.

The interior and the Main Chapel
The interior of the Cathedral is an example in perfection of design, ith its clean lines, and the original positioning of the pillars: the most remarkable feature however, is the wonderful harmony achieved in the proportions of all the elements employed. The architectural forms are notable for their lack of ornamentation, being left prepared ready for decoration; it was planned to do this in the same way as was done in the Main Chapel. This Chapel is quite unique, with its circular plan and the bold main arch, adapted to the dome, which is 45 metres in height. Here can be seen praying figures of the Catholic Sovereings, the sculptures being by Pedro de Mena. The statues of Adam and Eve in the upper part are by Alonso Cano. The interior of the dome is composed of two groups of superimposed Corinthian columns, with statues of the Apostles set around the first ledge. The spaces between the columns of the second group are adorned with seven large canvases depicting "Scenes from the Life of Our Lady", these being the work of Alonso Cano. Above these, we can admire the fine stained glass windows, portraying scenes of the Passion, this lovely series having been made in Flanders.

At the present time, the Choir is installed in the Main Chapel, having been situated in the central nave since the 16th Century.

The Cathedral Treasury
The Cathedral Treasury is on the left of the entrance, in the former Chapter Hall, and amongst the numerous artistic treasures which can be contemplate, we might mention the richly worked

29

vestments and adornments, Queen Isabella's Custody, seven Brussels tapestries, the 16th Century Chapter Cross, and the Maundy Thursday urn.

Other Chapels. The Sacristy

On leaving the Treasury, we pass, in order, the *capilla del Pilar*, the *Puerta de San Jerónimo* and the *capilla del Carmen y las Angustias*. The *Puerta del Perdón* is in the transept, and then we come to the *capilla de Nuestra Señora la Antigua*, where the 15th Century image, which tradition would have us believe came to Granada with the Catholic Sovereings, is greatly venerated. We continue on our way past a succession of other chapels, until we come to the Sacristy, the entrance to which was constructed by Siloé. The interior was built in the 18th Century, and here we may notice a 'Christ', by Montañés, and a picture of the "Annunciation", by Alonso Cano. A figure of the *Virgencita Inmaculada* is kept in a glass case, and is considered to be perhaps the finest work realised by Alonso Cano. On the right of the transept is the lovely original entrance to the Royal Chapel, now forming part of the Cathedral. Facing the Treasury we have another doorway similar to that of the old Chapter Hall, leading to a little museum.

The Alcaicería

After visiting the Royal Chapel and the Cathedral, it is a good idea to take a stroll through the little network of narrow streets which forms the ALCAICERÍA, the old Moorish silk market; this picturesque quarter has kept all its former character, and nowadays there are more than two hundred little shops in which wonderful examples of this particular branch of Grenadine craftsmanship are displayed.

The Palacio de la Madraza and the Corral del Carbón

Quite near the silk market, in the *plaza del Cabildo*, we come to the old PALACIO DE LA MADRAZA, a fine edifice built by the Arabs in the middle of the 14th Century, in the reign of Yusuf I; the fronting was especially lovely, being adorned with fine plasterwork on marble. This building was the seat of the first City Council convened in the time of the Catholic Sovereigns. In later epochs, the old Moorish palace suffered numerous alterations, Baroque embellishments being added and the façade opulently decorated with imitation mottled marble.

Among the more curious buildings in Granada, we ought to mention the so-called CORRAL DEL CARBÓN, an ancient *fondak*

The Cathedral. The Sacristy. "La Inmaculada", by A. Cano

The Royal Chapel.
"El Descendimiento",
by D. Bouts

which in Arab times served as both market place and inn. The outstanding feature of the interior is huge patio, with a pillar in the middle. Three storeys of galleries enclose the patio, each gallery containing a large number of very small rooms, such as are still to be seen in Arab countries. In appearance, this structure is of an extreme simplicity, and its main interest lies in the fact that it is the only remaining Arab *fondak* in Europe.

The Casa de los Tiros

Continuing our visit to the more notable buildings in Granada, we make our way to the CASA DE LOS TIROS, where the *Delegación de Turismo* is now installed. Here we have a typical Grenadine mansion, perfectly conserved in all its details; the house is surmounted by battlements, in the embrasures of which can be seen the culverins from which it takes its name. The edifice itself dates from the 16th Century, and used to belong to the Granada Venegas family, who for many centuries owned the *Generalife.* An interesting feature of the façade is the shield bearing the heraldic decive of a sword over a heart with the inscription *Él me manda* ("The heart commands me"). The interior is notable for its fine vestibule, where the painted Ghotic ceiling is particularly interesting. The patio is built according to the canons of Grenadine domestic architecture for this very important part of any residence. On the main floor, we can admire the *Salón Dorado,* adorned with statues of heroes and leaders, amongst which are the family shields, and again device "The heart commands me". The whole of this noble edifice is a veritable museum of Grenadine craftsmanship, and its atmosphere is still very much that of the residence of a noble family of Granada.

The Church of Santo Domingo

A short stroll from the *Casa de los Tiros,* we come to the CHURCH OF SANTO DOMINGO, which formed part of the *Monasterio de Santa Cruz,* a foundation that is now almost completely in ruins. A creation of the Catholic Sovereigns, we notice the frequency with which the emblems of these great monarchs and of Carlos V are repeated in the decoration of the church. The interior of the temple, Gothic and Renaissance in style, is the repository of great artistic riches, especially in its Main Chapel, where a late 17th century marble tabernacle particularly draws our attention. Praying figures of the Catholic Sovereigns, the creation of Alonso de Mena, together with four statues of priests of the

Orden de Predicadores, adorn the transept. In the front, we notice Baroque altars enriched with images of *Santa Escolástica,* and *San José,* and a lovely retable depicting scenes in the history of the Dominican Order; here too, can be admired a superb 15th century 'Christ'. On the left of the transept stands the retable of the *Virgen del Rosario,* and the Chamber of the rich ornamentation of Baroque artistry. The decorative theme of the antechamber is based on the Battle of Lepanto [1]. Of the remaining chapels, we ought to mention the alabaster image of the *Virgen de la Esperanza,* a greatly venerated figure which enjoys a reputation for achieving miracles; the image of the *Señor de la Sangre;* the bust of *La Magdalena,* and a number of paintings by Ambrosio Martínez, Gómez de Valencia, Juan de Sevilla, Atanasio Bocanegra and Pedro de Raxis.

The Monasterio de San Jerónimo

The MONASTERIO DE SAN JERÓNIMO is another of the edifices which must be counted among the architectural treasures of Granada. Begun in the first part of the 16th century, its Main Chapel was destined to be the last resting place of the mortal remains of the *Gran Capitán,* Gonzalo de Córdoba, and of his wife doña María Manrique. Among the first great artists who directed the building of this famous pile we find the name of Jacobo Florentino, *el Indaco,* at whose death the work of construction was placed in the hands of Diego de Siloé. The superb iron grilles which formed one of the chief decorative features of this church, together with its treasures, were all lost when the sacred pile was sacked during the Napoleonic invasion, the temple remaining in ruins until the beginning of the present century, when it was decided to carry out a complete restoration so that future generations might also admire this peerless example of Spanish Renaissance creative inspiration. The façade is a faithful reflection of Siloe's work, and is adorned with a shield and anagrams of the Catholic Sovereigns, and with busts of St. Peter and St. Paul. Towards the end of the 16th century, work was put in hand on the construction of the fronting, its design being entrusted to Díaz de Navarrete and Pedro de Orea; it is here that a fine statue of St. Jerome, the titular Saint, can be admired. On entering this temple, one is at once struck by its spaciousness and its well planned proportions, achieved by the use of a single nave, the

[1] The Battle of Lepanto resulted in a great victory for the forces of the Holy League — Venice, the Papal States, Genoa and Spain — against the Turkish fleet (1571).

The Cathedral. Capilla de la Antigua

The Lonja and the Royal Chapel

head of which is semi-octagonal. The great retable in the Main
Chapel is the result of a close and happy collaboration among
a number of artists; principally designed by Pedro de Orea, the
lovely carvings are the work of Diego de Navas, while Gaviria
realised the sculptures, and Pedro de Raxis was responsible for
the paintings. Here too, we can contemplate the praying statues
of the *Gran Capitán* and his wife. This famous old temple was
originally the repository of a magnificent painting —*Entierro de
Cristo*— by Jacobo Florentino, *el Indaco*, which can now be seen
displayed in the *Palacio de Carlos V.*

The Hospital de San Juan de Dios
Yet another of the noteworthy Renaissance buildings to be
admired in Granada is the HOSPITAL DE SAN JUAN DE DIOS, a place
that is known for its fine fronting, worked in Elvira marble by
Cristóbal de Vilches, and for the lovely Doric columns supporting
the arches in the cloisters. Adjoining the hospital, we have the
Baroque CHURCH, where is a richly decorated chamber in which
are conserved the pilgrim's staff, scrip and other treasured relics
of St. John of God, as well as the Saint's mortal remains, which
rest in a silver urn.

The University
A place with a great cultural tradition, the UNIVERSITY OF GRA-
NADA was funded in the 16th Century, and is now installed in
a notable17th Century Baroque edifice, where two Doric patios
are worthy of our attention; in addition to this fine building,
the Botanical Gardens, the Church of Santos Justo y Pastor,
and the College of San Bartolomé y Santiago all belong to the
University also.

The Temple of Nuestra Señora de las Angustias
Devotees of Baroque art will find a visit to the TEMPLE OF NUES-
TRA SEÑORA DE LAS ANGUSTIAS especially satisfying, this being one
of the most sumptuously decorated religious edifices in Granada;
one of tho outstanding features is the churrigueresque chamber
where stands the image of *Nuestra Señora de las Angustias,* a
figure of the Virgin which is deeply venerated by the people
of Granada.

The Cartuja
The CARTUJA, set amidst surroundings of breathtaking beauty,
is one of the most important religious monuments in all Granada.

with that of a certain Moorish princess. Nevertheless, *Macarena* comes from a Latin root, and according to an archaeologist, Collantes de Terán, it is derived from "Macarius", meaning the owner of a country villa and its adjoining lands, outside the city walls, in the time of the Romans.

The Walls and the Hospital de la Sangre

Now we can regard the proud ruins of the WALLS, still attempting to hold off the ravages of time and the choking grasp of the ivy which everywhere is slowly smothering them. Setting out from the *Puerta Macarena,* and going as far as the Chapel of *San Hermenegildo,* facing the Capuchine convent, we can pass seven towers which are still preserved. Historians refer to the rebuilding of these walls by Julius Cæsar, and to the restoration carried out by the *almorávide* and *almohade* Arabs, which are what we can see today.

In some stretches of these walls conservation works have just been carried out, the embattlements have been put back to their place, general cleaning and embellishment have contributed to provide us a view of perfect harmony.

Two great Sevillians, doña Catalina de Ribera, and her son, the first marqués de Tarifa, themselves met the cost of constructing the HOSPITAL OF THE FIVE WOUNDS, OR HOSPITAL DE LA SANGRE, the huge stone mass we notice as soon as we pass throught the *Puerta Macarena.* Work was begun on this great project about the middle of the 16th Century, the plans drawn up by Gaínza, the Cathedral architect, being based on Greco-Roman architecture; the finished edifice comprised four façades, with a magnificent fronting of white marble. The church is another creation of the master craftsman responsible for the bell tower of the *Giralda,* Hernán Ruiz, and for sheer beauty it must be considered as one of his finest achievements.

The Virgen de la Esperanza in San Gil Church

Before drawing this itinerary to its close, let us offer our prayers to the tenderest of the Macarenas, NUESTRA SEÑORA DE LA ESPERANZA, in her basilica, which lies in the very shadow of the *Arco.* Although this temple was destroyed in 1936, the piety and generosity of the people of Seville, and of their countless American friends, made it possible to rebuild the sacred pile in all its former splendour.

34

The Church of Santa Ana

The CHURCH OF SANTA ANA, situated in the plaza which bears its name, was erected on the site of an Arab mosque, its design being the work of Diego de Siloé; the tower is one of the most typical examples of the Grenadine style, and is extensively decorated with Mudéjar elements. Passing on to the interior, the nave displays a particulary fine specimen of Spanish panelling, and in one of the chapels we notice the greatly venerated *Dolorosa*, by Mora, as well as other interesting painting and religious sculptures.

The Bañuelo

The narrow little streets around this temple abound with notable edifices, such as the PALACIO AGREDA, the RESIDENCE OF THE CONDES DEL ARCO, and the BAÑUELO, the old Moorish baths, with their patio leading to the bathing rooms. If we make our way along *calle de Zafra* we can observe the CONVENT OF SANTA CATALINA, and a few steps farther on we come to the CHURCH OF SAN JUAN DE LOS REYES, where a Moslem minaret was converted into a Gothic tower.

The Casa del Castril *and the Provincial Archaeological Museum*

As we continue along the *carrera del Darro,* we reach the CASA DEL CASTRIL, a Grenadine mansion belonging to Hernando de Zafra, which now houses the ARCHAEOLOGICAL AND FINE ARTS MUSEUM, a place of considerable interest for those who enjoy studying collections of prehistoric, Iberian, Roman and Visigoth remains, or for visitors who find pleasure in contemplating paintings by artists of the Grenadine School.

The Casa del Chapiz

The *carrera del Darro* brings us to a delightful road, *paseo de los Tristes,* up which we make our way to the *Albaicín* over the *cuesta del Chapiz;* close by is the School of Arab Studies, now installed in the CASA DEL CHAPIZ, a Moorish building in which Arab and Christian elements are intermingled in the true Grenadine fashion. The patio, with its large pool, calls to mind the enchanted courtyards of the Alhambra and the *Generalife.* Now we are indeed in completely Moorish surroundings here among the gardens and orchards, with the little villas and the minarets of ancient mosques, now converted into Christian churches, and our way takes us along narrow little alleys between limewashed walls, with every now and then a building of two.

The Palace of Daralhorra

Wherever we go in this quarter we come across Moorish houses, and occasionally a palace, such as that of DARALHORRA, the home of Boabdil's [1] mother, of which many remains can still be observed. On arriving at the tiny *plaza de San Nicolás* we would do well to pause, so that we may enjoy an unforgettable sight as we regard the wonderful panorama of the Alhambra and the *Generalife,* with the snowy peaks of the *Sierra* far away in the distance.

The Albaicín quarter

The whole of the *Albaicín* quarter is made for the enjoyment of Nature; lying on the slope of a hill, its gardens are separated one from another, and from any point one can look out over broad vistas that delight the senses. The more modest appearance of the houses and villas in the *Albaicín* is a direct link with the Arab epoch and the character of those Moorish inhabitants, who alway display greater interest in natural values than in constructive riches. The influence of such a spirit can be seen even today in this quarter, where the people live in happy community, without any apparent class distinctions or sumptuous ostentation. Here indeed is a perfect urban organisation, where the streets breathe the same spiritual tranquillity as the private gardens, and where the public spaces are inevitably gathering places for groups of friends; wherever one cares to turn, there is alway the glorious sight of mases of flower and greenery, set off to perfection by the dazzling white of limewashed walls.

The numerous little Moorish houses we come across are inhabited just as in the days of Arab splendour, their original aspect hardly changed by any later alterations that may have been effected. We should like to mention a few of these houses, so that our visitor may really see them for himself. One of the most wonderfully preserved is at Nº 2 *calle de Yanguas,* while others which are also worthy of attention are Nº 12 *calle de San Luis,* Nº 27 *calle del Soto,* Nº 22 *calle de Fátima,* and Nº 1 *calle de Ceniceros,* this last an Arab building which was partially altered in the 16th Century, and that of *calle del Horno de Oro.*

The Sacromonte and the Gipsies

Once we have explored the *Albaicín,* we ought to make good

---

[1] Mohamed Abu Abdallah, known to the Castilian chroniclers as Boabdil *el Chico,* Emir of Granada, which place he surrendered to the Catholic Sovereings in 1492.

use of the opportunity to visit the gipsy quarter of the SACRO-MONTE; to really appreciate the position and the atmosphere of the caves it is better to go there during the day, but to experience the thrill of the *zambra* only a nocturnal visit will do. To reach this quarter, we must retrace our steps as far as the CASA DEL CHAPIZ, where the road to the *Sacromonte* begins. Once we come to the caves, we can indeed see what it can be to live close quarters with Nature; this necessity in the Grenadine character of always havings access to a broad vista is again apparent here, where the prickly pear trees, and the agaves are sharply silhouetted against the fresh whiteness of the limewashed caves. The pulsating vitality of the gipsies is seen to its best advantage in this spontaneous, somewhat wild setting. Each family has its cave, usually consisting of a sizeable space at the front, the scene of ordinary daily life, and the stage for the exhilarating celebration of gipsy dances; the walls are carefully limewashed and brilliantly polished copper utensils and adornments hanging there gleam in the firelight, adding to the witchery of the spectacle at night. As the need arises, further rooms and apartments are excavated from the living rock behind the main front caves.

The particular temperament of the gipsies gives rise to a complete spontaneity in their more spectacular demonstrations, and there is no doubt whatever that they are possessed by some strange inner urge to dance, even though in some respects it has now developed into a sort of financial enterprise. The *zambra* has a ritual background, its origins lost in the mists of antiquity, its development marked by alien influences brought from remote countries by this strange race. To watch the almost feverish rhythms of this dance for the first time in the bewitching atmosphere of the *Sacromonte,* a dance that is faceted with all the colour and vitality which are an essential part of the gipsy character, is a memorable sight and a stirring experience. The women sway and turn through all the complicated steps to the throbbing rhythm of the guitar and the sharp counterbeat of the castanets, while all the time the bystanders keep up a steady accompaniment of carefully timed clapping, the tempo increasing as the dance grows to its wild climax.

We think it is a good idea to include a short chapter compiled by José María Fontana, a man who knows Granada and the Sierra intimately, and who is besides more than qualified to write of the delights of the Grenadine cuisine.

SIERRA NEVADA. LAS ALPUJARRAS. COSTA DEL SOL

Up to the Pico de Veleta. *Eternal snows*

Why not go by car to the top of the highest mountain in Spain, at an altitude of 3400 metres. A road which goes through Cenes, winds past scenes of wild grandeur, rising up to bare rocks and outcrops, making an ascent of 2500 metres in less than 35 kilometres travelling, to reach a point just a short distance from the *Pico de Veleta.* From there you can look out over half Spain — lakes, perpetual snows, and, with a little luck, a group of wild goats *(Capra hispanica* or *Ibex),* will all combine to delight your senses. The solitary grandeur of this vast tapestry, the dark gashes of the gorges where the rivers surge forth to the daylight, and the impressive magnitude of the panoramas to be contemplated, either during the ascent or seated tranquilly at the summit, all display the majestic wonder of Nature.

As you look down from the Veleta, you will be regarding a privileged land, where in 50 kilometres you can experience all the varying climates, from the eternal snows of the *Corral del Veleta* to the perpetual tropics of the *Costa del Sol.* In a single day you can ski on a warm June morning (sometimes even in July and August too), and bathe at dusk among exotic flowers and sub-

39

tropical fruit trees. The excursionist will find that the various Grenadine mountaineering clubs are only too pleased to help him as much as possible, and he may even come across pleasans companions to go with him on longer trips, spending days at a time above the 3000 metres line, camping beside clear mountain lakes.

The inns stay open all winter for the skiers' use. There has been performed, near the Peñones de San Francisco, in a zone situated at 2500 metres of altitude, a vast project of constructions of the important winter field *Solinieve* which has the most meridional ski tracks of Europe.

An interesting trip for geologists, entomologists and botanists too, this excursion is a thrilling experience for anybody who has a good vehicle available.

Towards Motril. Sun-bathed country

A short way out from Granada, the road begins to descend towards Motril, winding through the *Valle de Lecrín,* among citrus groves and olive groves, everywhere the brilliant colours of the flowering oleanders and the air sweet with the fragrance of the orange trees and the flowers. Once past Vélez Banaudalla, a pretty little town with an Arab castle, and after breasting a short rise, you go through the tunnel which brings you out to the coastal belt, where the delicate pink and white of the almond blossom stretches down to the dazzling blue of the *Mare Nostrum.* In this region can be seen mile after mile of carnations and sugar canes, and jasmine and bougainvillea are bloom the whole year round. The Phoenicians, merchants and fond of good living, came in search of the silver which lies in these mountains and stayed to enjoy the gentle, unhurried life of the coast, where they could catch the fish with which they prepared a rich sauce known as *garum.* The sailing craft still conserve the lines of past ages, and the benevolent climate permits of excursions by sea. Ashore, you can laze under banana trees and persimmons, while far inland the pure snow on the *Sierra* shines dazzlingly white in the sun. Starting out from the small port of Motril, 9 kilometres along the road is Salobreña, a pretty little place, and 13 kilometres farther on lies Almuñécar, a delightful town that is the favourite summer resort of the Grenadines and an agreeable watering place in winter. The coast road continues amid ever changing scenery to Málaga, some 80 kilometres from Almuñécar.

The Cartuja. The Sacristy

The Cartuja.
Detail of the Tabernacle

The Alpujarras

The *Alpujarras* lie along the southern slopes of the *Sierra Nevada*. First of all, you follow the road to Motril which descends the *Valle de Lecrín,* and at *Venta de las Angustias* you turn off to the left. A region that is abundantly watered and carefully cultivated, the rich fields of maize and potatoes and the names of the villages at times recall Galicia; these communities were more or less completely isolated from the rest of the province for many years, and they still maintain a traditional form of life. Lanjarón, with its shaded walks, its hotels and its spa (recomended for liver ailments), is a fine centre for excursions and an ideal place for a rest.

GRENADINE CULINARY ARTS

The strong dishes
In the culinary arts, Granada reveals itself as a truly exceptional world. Just as in all other branches of its art, here too the great diversity of climates governing the Grenadine region have played an important part in the development of a native cuisine.

In all the better establishments in Granada, and even in the little country inns nearby, you can find such savoury dishes as a sort of black pudding and a *Sacromonte* omelet. As a noted gourmet once remarked, perhaps the most complex dish ever invented is the omelet, as cooks in widely separated countries, have at all times experimented with new, exotic combinations, so that by now it is almost impossible to discover an omelet that can be relished as being entirely different from all others. And yet, in Granada this unexpected pleasure awaits the appreciative palate, where one of the most sought after specialities of the cooks of the region is a delicious mixture of brains, entrails and fresh peas, tossed together with red peppers and fine slices of potato; this savoury concoction is folded into an omelet, making a truly appetising dish. Another variety consists of sweetbreads, chicken liver and kidneys, cooked over a quick fire in white wine to which a bouquet of herbs has been added; as a filling for a French omelet this in insuperable. When it comes to meat, chicken is probably the most tempting of all Grenadine dishes; the cooks of this ancient Moorish city have thought out so many succulent main

41

courses based on this common fowl that it would be impossible to mention them here. Let us simply say that whether it is served hot or cold, a plate of chicken in Granada is indeed food for the gods. In springtime you should not fail to try the broad beans for which this part of Spain is famous; seasoned with a finely balanced mixture of onions, tomatoes and artichokes, the flavour of the beans delicately brought out by a bouquet of herbs, with a couple of lightly poached eggs, this simple country dish is transformed into food that satisfies the most demanding taste.

An important feature of the Grenadine cuisines is the immense variety of almond soups; these rather unusual soups are based on a handful of almonds, which are first of all fried, and afterwards pounded in a mortar with a seasoning of peppers, caraway seeds, saffron and parsley, a piece of fried bread being added to give more body to the concoction. A few drops of vinegar serve to bring out the slightly piquant flavour to the full. Yet another product for which Granada is renowned is the superb Trevélez ham, cured in the little village from which it gets its name; two or three rashers of this ham served with broad beans make an appetising dish after a day's walking.

Sweetmeats and other specialities
As might be expected in a people with such a deeply rooted Moorish tradition, the confection of temping sweetmeats is something in which the Grenadines excel. In addition to all manner of dainties which are purely Arab in origin, Granada is famous also for the delicacies created by cloistered nuns. Let us mention some of the outstanding sweet dishes made in this region: fancy bread from Alfajar, a Grenadine village where the water has peculiar qualities which impart a delicacy of texture and flavour to even the most ordinary bread; *empanadillas de Santa Catalina,* a delicious sort of patty; syrups and candied fruits prepared by the *Comendadoras de Santiago; dulces de Santa Isabel,* a type of sweetmeat that simply melts in the mouth, and the famous creations of the *Hermanas Recogidas,* based on egg yolks. In the farms of the *Sierra* the women prepare a preserve which consists of slices of pumpkin and green fruits, cooked in honey.

We have tried to summarise the outstanding specialities of the Grenadine cuisine in a few brief paragraphs, but any visitor who can appreciate fine cooking and who goes exploring for himself in and around the city is certain to come across countless other tempting dishes. And fort those with time to make a trip to the

Village and typical landscape of La Alpujarra

View of the Albaicín
from the Alhambra

Almuñécar, on the Costa del Sol

the former is especially notable for the wonderful reliefs depicting the Birth of the Saviour; worked to a degree of classical purity, these are but another example of the superb craftsmanship of Montañés, who also carved the sepulchral statues of the founders and their wives, to replace the original effigies. Also worthy of particular attention is the Mudéjar style fronting of fine brickwork, against a background of polychromed tiles; this is a very characteristic type of decoration, of which the outstanding specimen is the one of Santa Paula. The patios of this monastery are veritable monuments of Mudéjar architecture, the *Patio de los Muertos* being notable for its tiled socles; the *Patio de los Evangelistas* is even more interesting however, with its wonderful murals, painted with a technique used before oils were known, and done entirely in red, black, yellow, white and ochre. The great patio dates from the 16th Century. The monastery of *San Isidoro del Campo* was occupied by Cistercian and Hieronymite communities successively. Recently the Hieronymite friars have again taken over the cenobium, now notably restored and fitted up especially in the part of its cloister. Thus we enjoy an easier visit with better information, and on the other hand the conservation of the monument that was practically abandoned, is guaranteed.

Castilleja de Guzmán. *Prehistoric archaeology*

On our way back, we should go up to the UNIVERSITY RESIDENCE OF SANTA MARÍA DEL BUEN AIRE in Castilleja de Guzmán, on the verge edge of the scarp formed by the plateau of the *Aljarafe*. An aristocratic mansion set in lovely gardens, the most attractive feature of this Residence is that it is also a superb vantage point, from which we can contemplate the Guadalquivir Plain stretching away into the distance and enjoy sweeping panoramas over Italica and Seville. The megalithic monuments constitute an archaeological richness of this region. LA CUEVA DE LA PASTORA and the tumulus of MATARRUBILLA (Valencina), the latter, the more distant, at five kilometres from Castilleja de Guzmán. These are two tombs, that is, underground caves, of the Eneolithic Age or the Copper Age. When excavating some dolmens they were discovered by Hugo Obermaier. As both monuments are situated away in the open country a visit certainly is not very comfortable for the tourist.

of the Alhambra; the *Cristo de los Gitanos,* borne up among the narrow streets of the *Albaicín* and the *Sacromonte,* to the accompaniment of the wailing chants of the gipsies —such aspects of the rites associated with Holy Week cannot be witnessed anywhere else in Spain.

The Feast of Corpus Christi is a time of rejoicing, when the people of Granada give themselves up completely to merrymaking; the air is sweet with the perfume of summer flowers and the fragrance of incense, and the city is resplendent with light and colour. From the 20th until the 30th June, the illuminated magnificence of the *Generalife* calls to mind the stories of the Arabian Nights, for it is in this enchanted setting that the International Festival of Music and Dancing casts its magic spell over the beholders, stirring the imagination to dream of past splendours of Old Granada.

HOTELS

DE LUXE CATEGORY

ALHAMBRA PALACE - Alhambra
NEVADA PALACE - Ganivet, 5

1st. Class A

BRASILIA - Recogidas, 1
KENIA - Molinos, 59
VICTORIA - Puerta Real, 3
WASHINGTON IRVING - Alhambra

1st. Class B

CARLOS V - Plaza de los Campos, 10
INGLATERRA - Cetti Merien, 4
LOS ANGELES - Escoriaza, 15
PARADOR DE SAN FRANCISCO - Alhambra
RALLYE - Camino de Ronda, 97
RESIDENCIA ANACAPRI - Abenamar, 12
SUDÁN - Acera del Darro, 18
VERSALLES - Solarillo de Gracia, 7

2nd. Class

ALCÁZAR - Puente Castañeda, 6
CASABLANCA - Frailes, 3
LA PERLA - Reyes Católicos, 2
LOS FAISANES - Duquesa, 35
LOS TILOS - Plaza Bibarambla
MANUEL DE FALLA - Antequeruela Baja, 16
MONTECARLO - Acera del Darro, 2
NIZA - Navas, 16
SACROMONTE - Plaza Lino, 3
UNIVERSAL - Recogidas, 20
ZAIDA - Acera del Darro, 17
ZOCAY - Avda. Andaluces, 7

3rd. Class

CANTÁBRICO - Navas, 26

CONTINENTAL - Alhóndiga, 8
REGINA - Acera del Darro, 4
SUIZO - Acera del Darro, 26
VICTORIANO - Navas, 24

PENSIONS

DE LUXE CATEGORY

AMÉRICA - Real de la Alhambra, 57
COLOMBIA - Antequeruela, 13
GRAN VÍA - Gran Vía, 13
HISPANIA - Puerta Real, 1
LISBOA - Plaza del Carmen, 29
SORRENTO - Gran Vía, 4
SUECIA - Cuesta Molinos

1st. Class

ALAMEDA - Acera del Casino, 13
BRITZ - Cuesta de Gomérez, 33
CALIFORNIA - Cuesta de Gomérez, 33
CANTÁBRICA - Sierpe Baja, 94
COLOMBIA - Antequeruela Baja, 13
FABIOLA - Ganivet, 3
HOSTAL DUQUESA - Duquesa, 8
IBERIA - Cuesta de Gomérez, 1
LANDAZURY - Cuesta de Gomérez, 18
PUERTA REAL - Acera del Darro, 10
REINA ISABEL - Mesones, 1 (Rooms only)
REY FERNANDO - Acera del Darro, 36
SEVILLA - San Sebastián, 12
VALENCIA - Alhóndiga, 13
ZACATÍN - Ermita, 9

2nd. Class

ALASCIO - Tra. Andaluces, 16
ALIATAR - Acera del Darro, 5
ABENAMAR - Abenamar, 10
BETANIA - Alhóndiga, 7
BRASIL - Cardenal Mendoza, 10
CENTRAL - Mesones, 21

PRACTICAL INFORMATION SUPPLEMENT

TO THE GUIDE TO

GRANADA

Ducal - Sacristía de S. Matías, 1
España - Acera del Casino, 13
Fermín - Navas 14 (Rooms only)
Florida - Príncipe, 2
Generalife - Plaza Mariana Pineda, 42
Imperial - San Antón, 2 - T. 23743
Julita - Párraga, 31 - T. 24704
Los Cármenes - I. Albéniz, 2
La Granadina - Párraga, 5
Meridiano - Angulo, 7 - T. 22981
Moles - Mesones, 39 - T. 23818
Montecarlo - San Antón, 14
Nuevo Colón - Párraga, 1
Progreso - San Antón, 87 - T. 22850
Regional - Navas, 6 - T. 22547
Robledo - Mesones, 4 - T. 21247
San Pedro - Campo Verde, 3
Términus - Av. Andaluces, 10
Venecia - Acera del Casino, 7
Villarrosa - Arriola, 7
Roma - Navas, 1
Nilo - Cuchilleros, 22
Muñoz - Mesones, 89

Los Angeles - Telephone 55
Paraíso (3rd. Class) - Telephone 22
Mesa (1st. Class) - Telephone 7
Royal - Telephone 6
Avenida (1st. Class) - T. 49
Pensión Ana Gálvez - Telephone 53
Pensión Astoria (2nd. Class) - T. 75
Continental Marruecos (2nd. Class)
Pensión Florida (2nd. Class) - T. 80
Iberia (2nd. Class) - T. 132
El Sol (2nd. Class) - T. 130
Central (3rd. Class) - Generalísimo, 21
Linares (3rd. Class) - A. Damas, 9

ALMUÑECAR

Sexi (1st. Class A) - San Cristóbal
Portamar (1st. Class B) - Puerta del Mar
Caribe (1st. Class) - Carretera Málaga
Mediterráneo (1st. Class) - Av. José Antonio - Telephone 55
Reinoso (2nd. Class) - Calvo Sotelo, 24
Residencia Montemar - Paseo San Cristóbal - Telephone 10

HOTELS AND PENSIONS IN THE PROVINCE

LANJARON

Andalucía Palace (1st. Class B)
Nuevo Palace (1st. Class B) - T. 8
Andalucía (2nd. Class) - T 15
España (2nd. Class) - Telephone 11
Del Castillo (2nd. Class) - T. 120
Malagueño (2nd. Class) - T. 12
Miramar (2nd. Class) - Telephone 9
París (2nd. Class) - Telephone 56
Parque (2nd. Class) - T. 117
Salud (2nd. Class) - Telephone 19
Suizo (2nd. Class) - Telephone 10
Victoria (2nd. Class) - Telephone 14
Cristina - Telephone 95
El Dólar (3rd. Class) - Telephone 64

BAZA

Pensión Mariquita (2nd. Class)

CALAHONDA

Miramar (3rd. Class)

CASTELL DE FERRO

Mesón Castell (2nd. Class) - T. 8
Residencia Paredes - C. de Almería
Mar y Sol (3rd. Class) - C. de Almería

LA RABITA

Las Conchas (1st. Class)

3

MOTRIL

Costa Nevada (1st. Class A) - T. 751
Hotel Alhambra (2nd. Class) - T. 105
La Casita de Papel (2nd. Class)
    Carr. Málaga, 2 - Telephone 352
Hotel Duzman - Telephone 236
Hotel Mediterráneo (2nd. Class)
Motril (2nd. Class) - T. 418
Tropical (2nd. Class) - T. 505
Pensión Sierra Nevada - T. 441
San Antonio - Carr. Granada - T. 133

LA HERRADURA

La Caleta (3rd. Class)

GUADIX

Hotel Comercio (3rd. Class) - T. 2
Pensión Accitana - Telephone 90
Hostalis (2nd. Class) - T. 450
El Canario (3rd. Class) - Tribuna, 5

ALHAMA

Hotel Termas Martos (1st. Class B)

SIERRA NEVADA

Parador de Sierra Nevada (2450 m.)
Albergue Collado Sabina (2100 m.)
Albergue Universidad (2500 m.)
Hotel Sierra Nevada (2000 m.)
Hotel Santa Cruz (1500 m.)
Hotel Mulhacén (1.200 m.)

CAMPINGS

GRANADA

Reina Isabel (1.ª)

Los Álamos (1.ª)
Sierra Nevada (1.ª)
El Último (1.ª)
María Eugenia (2.ª)

PINOS GENIL

El Blanqueo (1.ª)

LA ZUBIA

Reina Isabel (1.ª)

GUADIX

Atala (2.ª)

MOTRIL

San Antonio (1.ª)

ALMUÑECAR

El Paraíso (1.ª)
El Pozuelo (1.ª)
Rincón de la China (2.ª)

CASTELL DE FERRO

Castell (1.ª)
Las Palmeras (2.ª)

RESTAURANTS

Coimbra - Campillo Bajo, 37
Jandilla - Puerta del Carbón, 7
Los Leones - Acera del Darro, 10
Los Manueles - Zaragoza, 2
Los Mariscos - Escudo del Carmen
Nueva Mayer - Rubio, 1
Parada - Avda. Calvo Sotelo, 2
Polinario - Real de la Alhambra
Victoria - Puerta Real, 5

TYPICAL RESTAURANTS

ALCAICERÍA - Oficios, 8

EL MESÓN - Plaza Gamboa, 15

LOS MÁRTIRES - Carmen de los Mártires (Alhambra)

PATIO ANDALUZ - Escudo del Carmen, number 10

SEVILLA - Oficios, 14

TYPICAL TAVERNS

BOBADILLA - Ctra. Santa Fe

EL ÚLTIMO VENTORRILLO - Ctra. Huétor Vega

ERNESTO - Ctra. de Sierra Nevada

LA MOSCA - Camino La Zubia, 1

LOS ROSALES - Ctra. de Jaén, 86

SAN FRANCISCO - Carretera de Pinos Puente

ZORAYDA - Camino del Sacromonte, 12

ZAMBRAS

CUEVAS DEL SACROMONTE

"ALBERTO" - Real de la Alhambra

ARTESANÍA SACROMONTE - Gomérez, 10

NIGHT-CLUBS

LOS ROSALES - C. de Jaén

TERRAZA ALBERTO - Real de la Alhambra

PARRILLA DEL HOTEL ALHAMBRA PALACE - Alhambra

PARRILLA DEL HOTEL CASABLANCA Frailes, 3

PARRILLA DEL HOTEL NEVADA PALACE A. Ganivet, 7

REY CHICO - Paseo del Padre Manjón

RÍO CLUB - Camino Pulianas

LA BOLERA - Ganivet, 7

JARDINES NEPTUNO - Camino de Ronda, 12

LA RUTA DEL SOL - Carretera Motril

BULLFIGHTING

BULLRING - Ava. del Dr. Olóriz

ADVANCE BOOKING OFFICE - Plaza Gamboa

HANDICRAFTS

ANTIGÜEDADES LINARES - Puerta del Vino-Alhambra

ARTESANÍA LINARES - Real de la Alhambra

ARTESANÍA LINARES REYES - Hotel Alhambra Palace

COMERCIOS DE LA ALCAICERÍA - Alcaicería (Embroidered tulles, marquetry)

TEJIDOS ARTÍSTICOS ARTEGRAN - I. Albéniz, 2, Grupo C (Alpujarran cloths)

TEJIDOS ARTÍSTICOS FORTUNY - Plaza Fortuny, 1 (Alpujarran cloths)

BANKS

BANCO DE BILBAO - Reyes Católicos, 24

BANCO CENTRAL - Gran Vía, 8

BANCO DE ESPAÑA - Gran Vía, 16

BANCO ESPAÑOL DE CRÉDITO - Reyes Católicos, 20

BANCO HISPANO-AMERICANO - Gran Vía, 1

BANCO HIPOTECARIO - Carrera del Genil, 21

BANCO POPULAR ESPAÑOL - Acera del Casino, 17

BANCO RURAL - Gran Vía, 15

5

Banco de Santander - Gran Vía, 8

Banco de Vizcaya - Plaza del Carmen, 4

Banco Mercantil e Industrial - Gran Vía, 6

Marsans, S. A. - Plaza Nueva, 9

Meliá - Reyes Católicos, 30 and Ganivet, 5

Wagons-Lits/Cook - Cuesta de Gomérez, 1

CONSULATES

Austria - Cuarto Real

Argentina - Gran Vía, 25 - T. 22530

Belgium - Los Mártires - Alhambra

Bolivia - Gran Vía, 41 - T. 21605

Colombia - Vistillas de los Angeles, 3

France - Los Mártires - Alhambra

Germany - Carret. de la Sierra, 38

Great Britain - Cruz de los Mártires Alhambra

Italy - Mesones, 2

Netherlands - Solarillo de Gracia, 1

Panama - Maestro Alonso, 1 - T. 21618

Peru - Plaza de los Campos, 10

Portugal - Santa Ana, 20

Uruguay - Santos, 2 - T. 22210

RENT-A-CAR

Atesa - Cuchilleros, 1

Avis-Rent a Car - Alhóndiga, 4

Gudelva - Pedro Antonio de Alarcón, 18

Martín Rull - Ganivet, 3

Meliá - Reyes Católicos, 30

TRAVEL AGENTS

A. T. E. S. A. - Cuchilleros, 1

Aymar - Ganivet, 2

Baixas - Navas, 9 - Telephone 21553

Cafranga - Escudo del Carmen

Chat - Placeta Cuchilleros, 15

OFFICIAL TOURIST OFFICE

Information Office of the Subsecretaría de Turismo - Casa de Los Tiros - Telephone 21022

MUSEUMS AND MONUMENTS

Archaelogical Museum - Casa del Castril-Carretera del Darro. Visiting hours: Winter: from 10 to 14. Summer: from 9 to 14

Archaelogical Museum - (Gran Capitán) - Carretera de Puliana. Visiting hours: Winter: from 10 to 13 and from 15 to 18. Summer: from 10 to 13 and from 16 to 19

Archaelogical Museum - Palacio de Carlos V (Alhambra). Visiting hours: Like Alhambra and Generalife

Provincial Museum of Fine Arts Palacio de Carlos V (Alhambra). Visiting hours: Like Alhambra and Generalife

Municipal Museum - Visiting: from 10 to 14

Museo Catedralicio - Catedral - Visiting hours: Winter: from 11 to 13 and from 15 to 18.30. Summer: from 11 to 13 and from 15.30 to 19.30

6

Museo Arte Granadino - Casa de los Tiros - Visiting: from 10 to 13 and from 16 to 19

Alhambra and Generalife

January: from 10 to 18

February: from 10 to 18.30

March: from 10 to 18.30

April: from 9.30 to 19

May: from 9 to 19

June: from 9 to 20.30

July: from 9 to 20.30

August: from 9 to 20

September: from 9.30 to 19.30

October: from 9.30 to 19

November: from 10 to 18

December: from 10 to 18

Church of Santa María de la Alhambra - Winter: from 10 to 14 and from 15.30 to 18. Summer: from 10 to 14 and from 16 to 19

Casa de los Tiros - Winter and summer: from 10 to 13 and from 16 to 19

Bañuelo (Moorih Baths) - Winter: from 10 to 14 and from 15 to 18. Summer: from 9.30 to 13.30 and from 16 to 20

Corral del Carbón - Winter: from 10 to 18. Summer: from 10 to 18.30

Cathedral - Winter: from 11 to 13 and from 15.30 to 18. Summer: from 11 to 13 and from 14 to 19

Royal Chapel - Winter: from 11 to 13 and from 15.30 to 18. Summer: from 11 to 13 and from 16 to 19.

Church of the Cartuja - Winter: from 10 to 13 and from 15 to 18. Summer: from 10 to 13 and from 16 to 19

Church of San Jerónimo - Winter: from 10 to 13 and from 15 to 19.30. Summer: from 10 to 13 and from 16 to 19

Chancellery - Winter: from 10 to 18. Summer: from 10 to 19

Arbey of the Sacromonte - Winter: from 10 to 12. Summer: from 10 to 19

University - Winter and summer: from 10 to 13 and from 15 to 19

Church of San Juan de Dios - Winter: from 10 to 12.30 and from 16 to 18. Summer: from 10 to 12,45 and from 16 to 19

Church of Nuestra Señora de las Angustias - Winter and summer: from 9 to 22

Santa Isabel la Real - Winter: from 10 to 12 and from 16 to 18. Summer: from 10 to 12 and from 16 to 18.30

Casa de las Pisas - Winter and summer: from 10.30 to 13.30 and from 15.30 to 18

TYPICAL FEASTS IN GRANADA

Holy Week - Splendid processions during all the week

Corpus Christi Feasts - They beguin the day before and last ten days

International Festival of Music and Dance - From June 20th to July 4th of every year

Majorca by Lorenzo Villalonga. **Iviza** by Arturo Llopis. **The Costa Brava** by Néstor Luján. **Barcelona** by "Jaime Miravall". **The Montserrat** by José María de Sagarra. **Tarragona** by José María Espinás. **Valencia** by Martín Domínguez Barberá. **Costa Blanca and Costa de la Luz** by José Luis Castillo Puche. **Madrid** by César González-Ruano. **Toledo** by Gaspar Gómez de la Serna. **The Escorial** by Luis Felipe Vivanco. **Avila** by Camilo José Cela. **Segovia** by the Marquis of Lozoya. **Salamanca** by Rafael Santos Torroella. **Burgos** by Fray Justo Pérez de Urbel. **Granada** by Francisco Prieto-Moreno. **Seville** by Rafael Laffón. **Cordoba** by Ricardo Molina. **Malaga and Costa del Sol** by José María Souvirón. **Cádiz, Jerez and Los Puertos** by J. M. Caballero Bonald. **Corunna** by Carlos Martínez-Barbeito. **Santiago de Compostela** by Ramón Otero Pedrayo. **Rías Bajas of Galicia** by José María Castroviejo. **Saragossa** by Luis Monreal. **Tenerife** by Carmelo García Cabrera. **Grand Canary** by Carmen Laforet. **The Basque Country** by Ignacio Aldecoa.

ANDAR Y VER Collection. Aspects of Spain

Bulls and Bullfighting by José Luis Acquaroni
Andalusian Dances by José Manuel Caballero Bonald

"ANDAR Y VER". GUIDES TO SPAIN
do not accept any advertisements. All
establishments mentioned are done so freely.